When Your Porcupine Feels Prickly

KATHY DeZARN BEYNETTE

Pomegranate kids

SAN FRANCISCO

Published by PomegranateKids®, an imprint of
Pomegranate Communications, Inc.
Box 808022, Petaluma, CA 94975
800 227 1428 | www.pomegranate.com

Pomegranate Europe Ltd.
Unit 1, Heathcote Business Centre, Hurlbutt Road
Warwick, Warwickshire CV34 6TD, UK
[+44] 0 1926 430111 | sales@pomeurope.co.uk

To learn about new releases and special offers from Pomegranate, please
visit www.pomegranate.com and sign up for our e-mail newsletter.
For all other queries, see "Contact Us" on our home page.

This product is in compliance with the Consumer Product Safety Improvement Act of 2008 (CPSIA). A
General Conformity Certificate concerning Pomegranate's compliance with the CPSIA is available on our
website at www.pomegranate.com, or by request at 800 227 1428.

Library of Congress Control Number: 2012938893

ISBN 978-0-7649-6318-6

Pomegranate Catalog No. A214
Designed by Gina Bostian

Printed in China
21 20 19 18 17 16 15 14 13 12   10 9 8 7 6 5 4 3 2 1

For Calvin and Camille

DOG + CAT

JUMP to attention when your dog says, "FOOD!"

To do any less would just be rude.

And always offer a choice to your cat:

"Would you prefer this? Perhaps you'd like that?"

Menu
Fish
Chips
Tacos
Shrimp
Cake

KathyBurnette

BEE

When your bee is feeling down,

maybe she should wear a crown.

Anytime I'm feeling blue,

nothing but a crown will do.

SKUNK

If someone brings your skunk a treat,

write a note; say, "That was sweet!"

Use your pencil, crayon, or pen,

and maybe they'll bring one again!

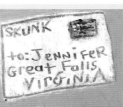

BIRD

Remove your hat when you talk to your bird

(though this may be contrary to what you've heard).

It shows that you trust him, it shows her respect;

it shows you don't think you'll be pooped on or pecked.

SHARK

If you make a rude remark,

I hope it won't be to your shark.

Don't say, "That's a stupid sweater,"

or "I like sharks, but whales are better."

Keep your shark relations happy!

Rudeness makes us all feel snappy.

SPIDER

Some things to know if your pet's a spider,

to make life sweeter for both of you:

Don't lie down for a nap beside her—

if you roll over, she'll end up goo!

And if your spider should go missing

while you're away at school or church,

do not call the spider shelter

'til you've done your own web search!

PENGUIN

After your penguin has taken a pee,

put down the seat, if he is a he.

Toilets are tricky for those who have flippers;

maybe that's why penguins never wear zippers.

GOAT

If your goat is being bad,

do not yell, and don't get mad.

Say, "I don't think you've been fair;

take a seat in the time-out chair."

Show him compassion, show him you care;

think of the times that you've sat there!

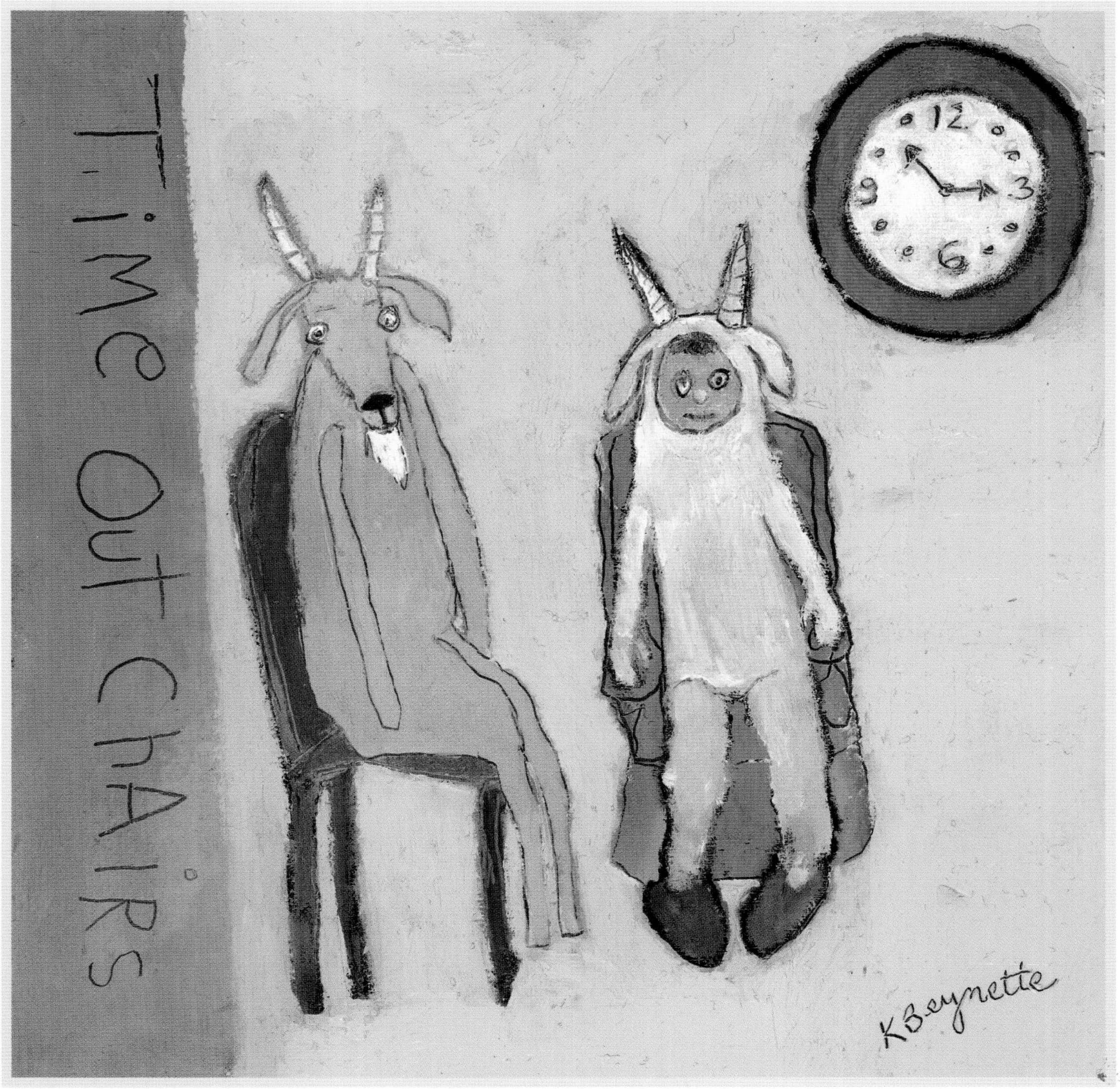
Time Out Chairs
12
3
6
9
K Beynette

COCKROACH

My cockroach is smart;

he's a survivor.

He won't take a ride

with any strange driver.

PONY

Your pony might tell you, by way of a dance,

he's thinking of nothing but changing his pants.

Open the door to let him inside,

and cover your eyes so he won't have to hide.

FLOUNDER

Ever since the day I found her,

I have worried 'bout my flounder.

She eats lots of tartar sauce,

but always she forgets to floss.

(PLEASE floss, Miss Fishy!)

TICK

If you are scared of being sick,

then don't adopt a pet deer tick.

One thing about them turns me off:

they never cover their mouths when they cough.

(Even with all those hands . . . I just don't get it!)

HIPPO

When your hippo wears something new,

say, "That color looks nice on you!"

If she asks, "Do I look fat?"

say, "I *never* would think that!"

RACCOON

Your raccoon won't come when you call,

or sit on your lap, or chase a ball.

Late at night, if you hear a crash,

it's probably him, raiding the trash.

YOU may think he's cute as a button;

I think he's just a little glutton.

Okay, I will admit he's neat;

I've seen him wash his hands to eat.

OWL

If your owl seems not as wise

as other owls of similar size,

don't insist he take a test;

find out what he loves the best.

Teach him in a friendly way

that work we love feels more like play.

LADYBUG

Treat your ladybug like a lady,

unless your ladybug is a man.

In *that* case, call him "Sir Lady"

and get along the best you can.

BULL

If your bull is a bully, don't be surprised;

it kind of goes with the name.

Don't try to shame him—you'll only inflame him;

just keep him away from the tame.

PELICAN

When I sniff a real bad smell, I can

always trace it to my pelican.

His breath makes my stomach queasy,

but he's so nice, I take it easy

and offer him a minty present.

For a moment, things are pleasant,

'til he says, "I only wish

your mints were flavored more like fish!"

MOUSE

Every mouse birthday should be celebrated

with freshly squeezed juice and cheese freshly grated.

Hire top chefs and fun party planners!

Use the best china; use your best manners.

Kathy
Bernette

BABOON

If you answer the phone and it's for your baboon,

say, "He's not here, but he's coming home soon."

And if there's a message, please write it down neatly;

take down the name and the number completely.

One thing that gets a baboon really riled

is when he calls back and is told he misdialed!

PORCUPINE

When your porcupine feels prickly,

don't assume that she is sickly.

Our vet told us not to worry:

porcupines are never furry.

CAT

My crazy cat Willie knows every rule,

but here is the thing that makes him so cool:

he knows it's okay if he makes a mistake;

sometimes the best rule is one you can break!

You cannot be perfect; you're sure to have flaws—

like food in your teeth, or dirt on your paws—

but they make you special, you and your pet.

They make you someone I'm glad to have met!

About the Author

Perhaps best known for her whimsical paintings inspired partly by children's art, Kathy DeZarn Beynette is also an accomplished writer of fiction and poetry. Her storytelling talent lends a richly narrative quality to her artwork, inviting us to see the world through her characters' eyes.

Kathy's creatures follow her wherever she goes, but the painting happens in a studio in Alexandria, Virginia.